William Bradford

**History of Plymouth Plantation**

William Bradford

**History of Plymouth Plantation**

ISBN/EAN: 9783742809742

Manufactured in Europe, USA, Canada, Australia, Japa

Cover: Foto ©ninafisch / pixelio.de

William Bradford

**History of Plymouth Plantation**

# HISTORY

OF

# PLYMOUTH PLANTATION.

BY

## WILLIAM BRADFORD,

THE SECOND GOVERNOR OF THE COLONY.

PURITANS GOING TO CHURCH.

*ARRANGED AND ANNOTATED FOR SCHOOLS.*

NEW YORK:

EFFINGHAM MAYNARD & CO., PUBLISHERS,

771 BROADWAY AND 67 & 69 NINTH STREET,

# LIFE OF WILLIAM BRADFORD.

WILLIAM BRADFORD was born in 1590 at Austerfield, an obscure town in Yorkshire, England. "Here and in some other places," writes Cotton Mather, to whom we are indebted for what is known of Bradford's early life, "he had a comfortable inheritance left him of his honest parents, who died while he was yet a child and cast him on the education, first of his grandparents, and then of his uncles, who devoted him, like his ancestors, unto the affairs of husbandry. Long sickness kept him, as he would afterwards thankfully say, from the vanities of youth, and made him the fitter for what he was afterwards to undergo. When he was about a dozen years old, the reading of the Scriptures began to cause great impressions upon him; and those impressions were much assisted and improved when he came to attend the ministry of Rev. Mr. Richard Clifton, not far from his abode; he was then also further befriended, by being brought into the company and fellowship of such as were then called professors. . . . Nor could the wrath of his uncles, nor the scoff of his neighbors, now turned upon him as one of the Puritans, divert him from his pious inclinations."

When about eighteen years of age, Bradford, with a company who had separated from the established church, went to Holland. He was twice arrested for having fled from England; but an explanation of his reasons secured his early release, and he was permitted to join his friends at Amsterdam. While there he became apprenticed to a Frenchman engaged in the manufacture of silks. On coming of age he promptly converted the property left him in England into money, and engaged in business for himself at Leyden. Here he continued until, with a portion of Mr. Robinson's church, he embarked in the Mayflower for New England.

The perils and hardships endured by the Pilgrims on this famous voyage are faithfully and graphically recorded in the History from which these selections have been made, and no doubt Bradford was an equal sharer in the many trials of the colonists on land. He was chosen the second governor of the colony in 1621, and continued in that office, with the exception of five years, until his death in 1657.

"He was a person for study as well as action; and hence, notwithstanding the difficulties through which he passed in his youth, he attained unto a notable skill in languages. . . . He was also well skilled in history, in antiquity, and in philosophy; and for theology, he became so versed in it, that he was an irrefragable disputant against the errors, especially those of Anabaptism, which with anxiety he saw rising in his colony; wherefore he wrote some significant things for the confutation of those errors." At length he fell sick, and so continued through a winter and spring, and died on the 9th of May following, in the sixty-ninth year of his age.

The opportunities which Governor Bradford had for writing the history of the Plymouth colony were superior to those of any other colonist; and although his duties as chief magistrate "would seem to afford him little leisure for writing, yet he thereby acquired an entire familiarity with every subject of a public nature in any way connected with the colony. This, taken in connection with the high character which he has always enjoyed, has caused this work to be regarded as of the first authority, and as entitled to take precedence of anything else relating to the history of the Pilgrims."

The history of the book is by no means uninteresting. After the death of the author the manuscript passed into the hands of his nephew Nathaniel Morton, who drew quite copiously from it for the facts in his "New England's Memorial." It afterwards came into the possession of Thomas Prince, who made use of it in his Chronological History of New England. On the death of

Prince it was left in the New England Library, in the tower of
the Old South Church, Boston. When Boston was occupied by
the British in 1775–76, the church was used by the British soldiers for a riding-school, and it is quite likely that Bradford's
manuscript history was among the spoils carried to Nova Scotia.
In 1855, the manuscript, which had long been given up for lost,
was found in Fulham Library, among a rare collection belonging
to the Bishop of London. How it ever got from Boston to London still remains a mystery.

Permission to copy the history was readily given, and in 1856
it was for the first time published in the Proceedings of the
Massachusetts Historical Society, and through the courtesy of
the librarian, Mr. Samuel A. Green, we are now enabled to pub-
lish these selections.

---

Inasmuch as the complete History covers a period of over
twenty-six years, it is necessarily too voluminous for school purposes. In attempting, therefore, to acquaint the pupils of our
schools with the trials encountered by the Pilgrim Fathers and
especially through the medium of this early American classic, it
has been necessary to abridge the narrative by omitting unimportant details of little or no interest to the general reader.
Care has been taken, however, not to omit any incident of historical value or anything that might shed light on the general
conditions in which the first settlers of Massachusetts were
placed. Because of the somewhat antiquated style of Governor Bradford's narrative, it has been thought best occasionally
to simplify it with more modern language, but as far as possible
the original has been retained; so that the reader may obtain a
knowledge not only of the history but of the literature as well.

"Next to the fugitives whom Moses led out of Egypt, the little shipload of outcasts who landed at Plymouth two centuries and a half ago are destined to influence the future of the world. The spiritual thirst of mankind has for ages been quenched at Hebrew fountains; but the embodiment in human institutions of truths uttered by the Son of Man eighteen centuries ago, was to be mainly the work of Puritan thought and Puritan self-devotion."—*James Russell Lowell.*

"Bradford and Winslow were both marked personages in that scene of interest unparalleled, that scene of few and simple incidents, just the setting out of a handful of not then very famous persons, on a voyage; but which, as we gaze on it, begins to speak to you as with the voices and melodies of an immortal hymn, which dilates and becomes idealized into the auspicious going forth of a colony, whose planting has changed the history of the world; a noble colony of devout Christians, educated, firm men, valiant soldiers, and honorable women; a colony, on the commencement of whose heroic enterprise the selectest influences of religion seemed to be descending visibly; and beyond whose perilous path are hung the rainbow, and the western star of empire."—*Rufus Choate.*

"That mixed and strong feeling, which we call love of country, and which is, in general, never extinguished in the heart of man, grasped and embraced its proper object here. Whatever constitutes *country*, except the earth and the sun, all the moral causes of affection and attachment which operate upon the heart, they had brought with them to their new abode. Here were now their families and friends, their homes, and their property. Before they reached the shore, they had established the elements of a social system, and at a much earlier period had settled their forms of religious worship. At the moment of their landing, therefore, they possessed institutions of government, and institutions of religion, and friends and families, and social and religious institutions, constituted by consent, founded on choice and preference, how nearly do these fill up our whole idea of country!"—*Daniel Webster.*

# PLYMOUTH PLANTATION.

## CHAPTER I.

### DISCONTENT OF THE PURITANS. DECISION TO GO TO HOLLAND.

IT is well known unto the godly and judicious, what wars and oppressions Satan hath raised, maintained, and continued against the saints, from time to time, and in one sort or other, ever since the first breaking out of the light of the gospel in our honorable nation of England. Sometimes it has been by bloody death and cruel torments; at other times by imprisonment, banishment, and other hard usage; as if he were loath that his kingdom should go down, the truth prevail, and the churches of God revert to their ancient purity and recover their primitive order, liberty, and beauty.*

---

* "In our country, the United States, there are many churches. If a person desires to be a Methodist, or a Baptist, or a Catholic, or an Episcopalian, or a member of any other church, he is at liberty to do so. Indeed, he may go to any church or may keep away from all churches, just as he pleases. This we call religious toleration. But toleration like this was not the state of things in England during the reign of James I. He belonged to what was, and is still, the Church of England. The laws of England were largely based upon the assumption that every Englishman belonged to the one Church in which it was declared 'was the only true worship.' Unlike the churches of our day and country, the Church of England was supported by taxes, very much as the army was supported. No other church received any such aid. In fact, no other church had any legal existence. If any body of persons wanted to build a church of another denomination, the laws said they must not.

"At that time there was a large number of persons in England who were called Puritans. They were very strict in their religious notions and mode of living. The most of them attended church as King James and the law

The one side labored to have the right worship of God established in the church, according to the simplicity of the gospel, without the mixture of men's inventions, and to be ruled by the laws of God's word, dispensed in those offices, and by those officers of pastors, teachers, and elders according to the Scriptures. The other party, though under many colors and pretenses, endeavored to have the episcopal dignity with their large power and jurisdiction still retained. But by the diligence of some godly and zealous preachers, and God's blessing in their labors, many became enlightened by the word of God, and had their ignorance and sins discovered[1] unto them.

These people became two distinct bodies or churches, and, on account of distance, did congregate severally; for they were of sundry towns and villages. In one of these churches (beside others of note) was Mr. John Smith, a man of able gifts, and a good preacher, who afterwards was chosen their pastor. But these afterwards falling into some errors in the Low Countries,[2] there (for the most part) buried themselves and their names.

But in this other church, which must be the subject of our discourse, besides other worthy men, was Mr. Richard Clifton, a grave and revered preacher, who by his pains and diligence had done much good, and under God had been the means of the con-

---

commanded, but they were in favor of a more simple form of worship, such a form as by its very simplicity would purify the church from, what they regarded, its follies and abuses. Hence their name, Puritans.

"Some Puritans went farther. Believing that it was impossible to effect any change in the church, supported as it was by law, king and a multitude of interests, they separated themselves entirely from it and set up another church, an independent church. Hence they called themselves Separatists or Independents. Unfortunately, they lived at a time when church persecutions were common. They could not meet except in secret. They were looked upon as rebels. One of their congregations, consisting of about three hundred persons, having been cruelly driven from place to place, resolved to go to Holland, where, they heard, ' was freedom of religion for all men.'"—*Anderson's New Grammar School U. S. Hist.*

---

[1] **Discovered.**—Revealed, made evident.

[2] **Low Countries.**—The Netherlands and Belgium.

version of many. And also that famous and worthy man Mr.
John Robinson, who afterwards was their pastor for many years,
till the Lord took him away by death. Also Mr. William Brewster,[3] a reverent man, who afterwards was chosen an elder of the
church and lived with them till old age.

But after these things they could not long continue in any
peaceable condition, but were hunted and persecuted on every
side, so that their former afflictions were but as flea-bites in comparison with those which now came upon them. Some were taken
and shut up in prison, the houses of others were beset and watched
night and day, and the most of them were fain to fly and leave
their houses, and the means of their livelihood. Yet these and
many other sharper things which befell them, were no other than
they looked for, and therefore they were the better prepared to
bear them by the assistance of God's grace and spirit.

Seeing themselves thus molested, and that there was no hope of
their remaining there, by a joint consent they resolved to go into
the Low Countries, where they heard there was freedom of religion for all men. So after they had continued together about a
year, and held their meetings every Sabbath in one place or another, exercising the worship of God amongst themselves notwithstanding all the diligence and malice of their adversaries,
seeing they could no longer remain in that condition, they resolved to go into Holland. This was in the years 1607 and 1608.

---

"An act of Parliament passed in the first year of Queen Elizabeth's
reign forbade all ministers to conduct public worship otherwise than according to the rubric.[4]

"A number of Puritan clergymen, some of whom were persons of distinction, refused to comply with this act, and they and their followers received the name of Non-Conformists."

---

[3] **William Brewster.**—One of the chief founders of Plymouth Colony. In the church at Leyden he had acted as ruling elder, and he discharged the same duties in the church at Plymouth until 1629, officiating as preacher twice every Lord's Day.

[4] **Rubric.**—*Meaning?*

## CHAPTER II.

### THEIR DEPARTURE INTO HOLLAND, AND THEIR TROUBLES THERE; WITH AN ACCOUNT OF SOME OF THEIR MANY DIFFICULTIES.

### 1608.

BEING thus compelled to leave their native soil, their lands and livings, and all their friends and familiar acquaintances, was much of an undertaking and thought marvelous by many. They regarded it an almost desperate adventure, and a worse misery than death, to go into a country they knew nothing about, where they must learn a new language, and get their livings they knew not how, it being a dear place[1] and subject to the miseries of war.[2] They were not acquainted with trades (by which the country doth subsist), and had only been accustomed to a plain country life and the innocent trade of husbandry. But these things did not dismay them, although they did sometimes trouble them.

Yet this was not all, for though they could not stay, yet they were not allowed to go. Their own ports and harbors were shut up against them, so that they were forced to seek secret means of conveyance, and to bribe and fee[3] the sailors, and to give extraordinary rates for their passages. Furthermore, they were often betrayed, and both they and their goods intercepted and surprised,[4] and they thereby put to great trouble and expense, of which I will give an instance or two.

A large company of them purposed getting passage at Boston,[5] in Lincolnshire, and for that object had hired a ship, and

---

[1] **Dear place.**—Expensive to live in.

[2] **Miseries of war.**—The war with Spain, after a twelve years' truce, was about to be renewed.

[3] **Bribe and fee.**—*Meaning?*

[4] **Surprised.**—Seized.

[5] **Boston.**—The name was originally St. Botolph's Town. See map.

made agreement with the master to be ready at a certain day to take them and their goods in at a convenient place where they would all be in readiness. Although he did not come to them on the day appointed, he came at length and took them away by night. But when he had them and their goods aboard, he betrayed them, having plotted with the searchers[6] and other officers;

who took them and put them into open boats, and there rifled[7] them of all their effects, then carried them back into the town and made them a spectacle to the multitude which came flocking on all sides to behold them. The result was that the greater part, after a month's imprisonment, were dismissed, and sent

---

[6] **Searchers.**—Officers appointed to examine outward-bound vessels to see that they did not carry prohibited goods.

[7] **Rifled.**—*Meaning?*

back to the places from which they came, but seven of the principals[8] were still kept in prison and bound over to the *Assizes.*[9]

The following Spring an attempt was again made at another place to cross over. They met with a Dutchman at Hull, and made an agreement with him, hoping to find him more faithful than their own countryman. Accordingly at the appointed time the women and children with their goods were sent to the place in a small bark, which had been hired for that purpose, and the men were to meet them by land. It so happened that they were there fully a day before the ship came, and the sea being rough, and the women sick, they persuaded the seamen to put into a creek close by, where the bark lay on ground at low water.

The next morning the ship came, but the bark was fast and could not stir until noon. In the mean time the ship's master, perceiving how the matter was, sent his boat to get the men whom he saw ready and walking about on the shore. But after the first load was got aboard, and the boat was ready to go for more, the master saw a great company of soldiers, both horse and foot, with bills[10] and guns, and other weapons; for the country was raised to capture them.[11] The Dutchman seeing this, and having a fair wind, weighed anchor, hoisted sails, and put out to sea.

The poor men who had just been taken on board were in great distress on account of their wives and children, whom they saw left without their help, and they themselves had no clothing, except that on their backs, nor hardly a penny about them—all they had being aboard the bark. They would have given anything they had to have been back again on shore, but it was all in vain; there was no remedy, they must sadly part.

---

[8] **Principals**.—*Meaning?*

[9] **Assizes.**—The principal sessions of the judges of the superior courts in the counties of England for the purpose of administering justice in the trial and determination of civil and criminal cases.

[10] **Bill.**—A sickle-shaped weapon.

[11] **Raised to capture them.**—The country was aroused to capture them.

Afterwards a fearful storm arose, and they were out fourteen days before they landed at their port.[12]

But to return to the others, whom we left on the shore. The rest of the men were in the greatest danger, and prepared to make their escape before the troops could surprise them. Those only remained who could be of the most assistance to the women. It was pitiful to see the condition of these poor women, weeping and crying; some for their husbands who were carried away in the ship; others not knowing what should become of them and their little ones; and still others in tears at seeing their little ones hanging about them, crying for fear, and shaking with cold. Thus captured, they were hurried from one place to another, and from one justice to another, till in the end the judges did not know what to do with them; for to imprison so many women and innocent children for no other cause but that they wanted to go with their husbands seemed to be unreasonable; and to send them home was as difficult, for they had no home to go to, having either sold or otherwise disposed of their houses and livings.

I might relate many other notable troubles which they endured in their wanderings both on land and sea; but I haste to other things. Yet I may not omit the results that followed, for by these public troubles, in so many eminent places,[13] their cause became famous. Though some few shrunk at these first conflicts and sharp beginnings, yet many more came up with fresh courage, and greatly animated others. So that in the end, notwithstanding all these storms of opposition, they all got over to Holland, some at one time and some at another, and some in one place and some in another, and met together again according to their desires, with no small rejoicing.

---

"The departure from England was effected with much suffering and hazard. The first attempt, in 1607, was prevented; but the magistrates checked the ferocity of the subordinate officers; and after a month's arrest of the whole company, seven only of the principal men were retained

---

[12] Port.—Amsterdam. | [13] Eminent places.—*Meaning?*

a little longer in prison. . . . Such was the flight of Robinson and Brewster, and their followers, from the land of their fathers. Their arrival in Amsterdam, in 1608, was but the beginning of their wanderings. They knew they were *pilgrims*, and looked not much on those things, but lifted up their eyes to heaven, their dearest country, and quieted their spirits."—*Bancroft.*

## CHAPTER III.

### SETTLEMENT IN HOLLAND, AND MANNER OF LIVING THERE.

HAVING come into the Low Countries, they saw many goodly and fortified cities, strongly walled, and guarded with troops of armed men. They heard a strange and uncouth language, and beheld the different manners and customs of the people, with their strange fashions and attires. But these were not the things they much looked on or considered; for they had work in hand, and another kind of war to wage. For though they saw fair and beautiful cities, overflowing with abundance of all sorts of wealth and riches, yet it was not long before they saw the grim and grisly face of poverty coming upon them like an armed man, with whom they must buckle and encounter, and from whom they could not fly.

When they had lived at Amsterdam about a year, Mr. Robinson, their pastor, and some others of best discerning, thought it was best to remove. For these and some other reasons they went to Leyden,[1] a fair and beautiful city. But, lacking that traffic by sea which Amsterdam[2] enjoys, it was not so beneficial for their outward means of living. Being thus settled after many difficulties they continued many years in a comfortable condition, enjoying much sweet and delightful society, and spiritual comfort under the able ministry and prudent government of Mr. Robinson, and Mr. William Brewster, who was an assistant to him.

[1] **Leyden.**— *Where?*                    [2] **Amsterdam.**— *Where?*

If at any time any differences arose or offenses broke out, as will sometimes happen amongst the best of men, they were always met and nipped in the head[3] betimes. Such was the mutual love and reciprocal[4] respect that Mr. Robinson had for his flock and his flock for him, that it might be said of him as it once was said of the famous Marcus Aurelius[5] and the people of Rome, that it was hard to judge whether he delighted more in having such a people, or they in having such a pastor.

But seeing it is not my purpose to treat of the several passages[6] that befell this people whilst they thus lived in the Low Countries, I will mention a particular or two to show the good acceptation[7] they had in the place where they lived. Though many of them were poor, yet there were none so poor but if they were known to be of the congregation, the Dutch would trust them in any reasonable matter when they wanted money. Because they had found by experience how careful they were to keep their word, and saw them so painstaking and diligent in their callings, that they would even try to get their custom,[8] and to employ them before others in their work, because of their honesty and diligence.

Again, the magistrates of the city, about the time of their departure, or a little before, in the public place of justice gave this commendable testimony of them. "These English," said they, "have lived amongst us these twelve years, and yet we never had any suit or accusation against them."

---

[3] **Nipped in the head.**—*Meaning?*

[4] **Reciprocal.**—*Meaning?*

[5] **Marcus Aurelius** (A.D. 161–180).— " Roman Emperor. He was the last of the good emperors. His 'Meditations' have made him known to posterity "—*Leighton's History of Rome.*

[6] **Passages.**—Passing events.

[7] **Acceptation.**—Reputation.

[8] **Custom.**—Trade.

## CHAPTER IV.

### SHOWING THE REASONS AND CAUSES OF THEIR REMOVAL.

AFTER they had lived in Leyden about eleven or twelve years, and sundry of them had been taken away by death, and many others had begun to be well stricken in years, the grave mistress Experience [1] having taught them many things, the prudent governors, with sundry of the sagest members, began both deeply to apprehend their present dangers and wisely to foresee the future, and think of timely remedy. And first they saw and found the hardness of the place and country to be such that comparatively few would come to them from England and fewer still would bide[2] it out, and continue with them. For many came to them, and many more desired to be with them, but could not endure the great labor and hard fare, with other inconveniences, which they underwent and were contented with.

They saw that although the people generally bore all these difficulties very cheerfully, and with a resolute courage, being in the best and strength of their years, yet old age began to steal on many of them, so that it was not only probably thought, but apparently seen, that within a few years they would be in danger of scattering, or of sinking under their burdens, or both. As Necessity[3] was a taskmaster over them, so they were forced to be such not only to their servants, but in a sort to their dearest children; which not a little wounded the tender hearts of many a loving father and mother, and produced likewise sad and sorrowful effects.

Though their minds were free and willing, yet many were so oppressed with their heavy labors that their bodies bowed under the weight and became decrepit in their early youth; the vigor of nature being consumed in the very bud, as it were.

---

[1] **Experience.**—*Meaning ?* | [2] **Bide.**—*Meaning ?* | [3] **Necessity.**—*Meaning ?*

Lastly (and which was not least), they had a great hope and inward zeal of laying some good foundation, for propagating and advancing the gospel of the kingdom of Christ in those remote parts of the world; yea, though they should be but even as stepping-stones unto others for the performing of so great a work. These, and some other similar reasons, induced them to carry out this resolution of removal.

The place they thought of was some one of those vast countries of America, which are fruitful and fit for habitation, where the natives are only savage and brutish men, who range up and down like wild beasts. When this proposition was made public and came to the consideration of all, it raised many favorable opinions, and caused many fears and doubts among them. If they should go, the hardships they would have to undergo might possibly cause the death of some or all of them. For they would be liable to famine, nakedness, and the want, in a manner, of all things. The change of air, diet, and drinking water would probably cause sickness and disease.

Those that should escape these miseries would be in constant danger of the savages, who are cruel, barbarous, and most treacherous, furious in their rage, and merciless where they overcome, not being content only to kill, but delighting to torment men in the most bloody manner. It was further objected that it would require greater sums of money to furnish supplies for such a voyage, and to fit them with necessaries, than their consumed estates would amount to. It was answered that all great and honorable actions are accompanied with great difficulties, and must be undertaken and overcome with corresponding courage. It was granted that the dangers were great, but not desperate; the difficulties were many, but not invincible. For though there were many of them likely to happen, yet they were not certain; and it might be that many of the things feared might never occur; others by provident care and the use of good means might, in a great measure, be prevented; and all of them, through the help of God, by fortitude and patience, might either be borne or overcome.

2

True it was that such attempts were not to be made and undertaken without good ground and reason; not rashly or lightly, as many have done from curiosity or hope of gain. But their condition was not ordinary; their purposes were good and lawful, and urgent; therefore they might expect the blessing of God in their proceedings. And even if they should lose their lives in this action, yet they might have comfort in the same, and their endeavors would be honorable. After many debates on the question, it was finally concluded by the greater part to put this design into execution, by the best means they could.

## CHAPTER V.

### Showing what Means they used in the Preparation for this Great Voyage.

And first, after humble prayer unto God for his direction and assistance, they consulted as to what particular place to decide upon. Some desired to go to Guiana,[1] or some other of the fertile places in those hot climates; others wanted to go to Virginia, where the English had already established themselves. Those who preferred Guiana asserted that the country was rich, fruitful, and blessed with a perpetual spring, where vigorous nature brought forth all things in abundance without any great labor or art of man. So that it must needs make the inhabitants rich, as less provision of clothing and other things would be required than in colder and less fruitful countries. The Spaniards, having much more territory than they could possess, had not yet planted there, nor anywhere very near the same.

For Virginia, on the other hand, it was objected that if they lived among the English who were settled there, or so near them

---

[1] One of the countries in northern part of S. America.

as to be under their government, they would be in great danger of being troubled and persecuted for the cause of religion—in fact quite as much so as if they lived in England, and it might be worse. And if they lived too far off, they should neither have help nor defense from them.

At length they came to the conclusion to live as a distinct body, under the general government of Virginia; and through their friends to sue to his Majesty [2] that he would be pleased to grant them freedom of religion; and they were put in good hope that this might be obtained by some great persons of good rank who were their friends. Two [3] were chosen and sent to England, at the expense of the rest, to solicit this favor. They found the Virginia Company very anxious to have them go there,[4] and willing to grant them a patent, with as ample privileges as they had or could grant to any, and to give them all the assistance they could. But it proved to be a much harder piece of work than they expected; for although much was done to bring it about, yet it could not be effected.

There were many of high standing who labored with the king to obtain the patent, and among these was one of the king's chief secretaries, and some even plead with the archbishop to grant their request, but without success. They prevailed far enough to sound his Majesty's mind that he would not molest them, provided they conducted themselves peaceably. And this was all the chief of the Virginia Company or any other of their best friends could do. Yet they persuaded them to go on, for they presumed they should not be troubled. And with this answer the messengers returned, and told what they had done.

---

[2] James I.

[3] Robert Cushman and John Carver. Robert Cushman was one of the business managers for the colony, and cared for their interests in England. He visited Plymouth once, in 1621. John Carver, a prominent man among the Pilgrims, was sent as agent to England to make plans for the departure of the whole company. First Governor of Plymouth Plantation, 1620. Died 1621.

[4] **There**.—Virginia.

Other messengers[5] were dispatched to conclude with the Virginia Company as well as they could, and to procure a patent with as good and ample conditions as they might by any fair means obtain, and to negotiate with such merchants and friends as had shown a desire to forward and take risks in this voyage.

---

## CHAPTER VI.

### PLANS PROPOSED BY LONDON MERCHANTS TO ASSIST IN THE UNDERTAKING.

AFTER this they concluded both what number and what persons should go with the first: for all who were willing to go could not get ready in so short a time; neither, if all could have been ready, would there have been means to have transported them all at the same time. Those that remained being the greater number required their pastor to remain with them, and as for other reasons he could not go, it was all the more readily yielded. The others then desired Mr. Brewster, the elder, to go with them, which was also conceded.

It was agreed on by mutual consent and covenant, that those that went should be an absolute church of themselves, as well as those that stayed;[1] as in such a dangerous voyage, and a removal to such a distance, it might happen that they should never meet again in this world. The proviso[2] was made that as any of the rest of the home church came over, or any of the others returned at times, they should be reputed as members without any further dismission or testimonial.[3] It was also promised to those who went first, by the body of the rest, that if the Lord gave them

---

[5] **Other messengers.**—Robert Cushman and William Brewster.

[1] **Stayed.**—Remained at home.

[2] **Proviso.**—A conditional agreement.

[3] **Dismission or testimonial.**—Church forms.

life and means and opportunity, they would come to them as soon as they could.

About this time, while they were perplexed with the proceedings of the Virginia Company, and were making inquiry about the renting and buying of shipping for their voyage, some Dutchmen [4] made them fair offers about going with them. Mr. Thomas Weston, [5] a merchant of London, came to Leyden about the same time, and after much conference with Mr. Robinson and others of their principal men, persuaded them to go on and not to meddle with the Dutch or to depend too much upon the Virginia Company; for if that failed, he and other merchants who were his friends, together, with their own means, would set them forth; and they should fear neither want of shipping nor money, for what they wanted should be provided.

Not so much for Mr. Weston as for the satisfying of such friends as he should get to venture in this business, they were to draw such articles of agreement, and make such propositions, as might better induce his friends to venture. Articles were drawn, and were shown unto him and approved by him, and afterwards sent to England by their messenger, Mr. John Carver, who, together with Robert Cushman, was to receive the moneys and make provision both for shipping and other things for the voyage, with this charge : not to exceed their commission, but to proceed according to the former articles.

About this time they heard both from Mr. Weston and others that sundry honorable lords had obtained a large grant from the king for the more northerly parts of the country, derived from the Virginia patent, and to be called New England. [6]

But now another difficulty arose; for Mr. Weston and some others who favored this course, either for their better advantage,

[4] The Dutch offered to transport the Pilgrims to the Hudson River without charge.

[5] **Thomas Weston.**—He pretended to be a friend of the Pilgrims, and proposed to organize the company to assist them, expecting, as they afterwards learned, to gain much money out of their risk.

[6] Mr. Weston advised the Pilgrims to alter their plans and ally themselves with the new company.

or rather for the better drawing on of others, as they pretended, would have some of those conditions that were agreed upon at Leyden altered.    The chief and principal differences between these and the former conditions were in these two points: that the houses, and improved lands, especially gardens and home lots, should remain undivided wholly to the planters at the end of seven years.    Secondly, that they should have two days in the week for their own private enjoyment, for the more comfort of themselves and families, especially such as had families.

-----

"Their greatest hardship was the compact with the merchants.    The Pilgrims were poor, and their funds were limited; they had no alternative, therefore, but to associate with others; and, as often happens in such cases, wealth took advantage of their impoverished condition.    By their instructions, the terms on which their agents were to engage with the merchants were definitely fixed, and no alteration was to be made without consultation. But time was precious; the business was urgent; it had already been delayed so long that many were impatient; and to satisfy the merchants, who drove their bargain sharply and shrewdly, some changes, compelled by the merchants, were made by Cushman, and by ten tight articles the emigrants were bound for the term of seven years."—*Hist. of Mass.* (Barry).

-----

## CHAPTER VII.

Departure from Leyden.    Arrival at Southampton, where they all met together and took in their Provisions.

At length all things were ready.    A small ship [1] was bought and fitted out in Holland, which was intended to help to transport them, and to stay in the country and attend upon fishing and such other things as might conduce to the good of the colony. Another [2] was hired in London, and all other things were got in readiness.    So being ready to depart, they had a day of solemn

[1] The Speedwell, a vessel of 60 tons.    [2] The Mayflower, a larger vessel of 180 tons.

humiliation, and a part of the time was spent in pouring out prayers to the Lord with great fervency, mingled with abundant tears.

The time having come when they must depart, they were accompanied by most of their brethren out of the city, to a town several[3] miles off, called Delft-Haven,[4] where the ship lay ready to receive them. So they left that goodly and pleasant city, which had been their resting-place nearly twelve years. When they came to Delft-Haven they found the ship and all things ready. That night was spent with but little sleep to the most, but with friendly entertainment and Christian discourse and other real expressions of true Christian love. The next day, the wind being fair, they went aboard, and their friends with them, where truly doleful was the sight of that sad and mournful parting. To see what sighs and sobs and prayers did sound amongst them, what tears did gush from every eye, what loving speeches pierced each heart, moved many of the Dutch strangers who stood on the wharf as spectators, and they could not refrain from tears. Yet comfortable and sweet it was to see such lively and true expressions of dear and unfeigned love.

But the tide which waits for no man called them away, though they were loth to depart. Their reverend pastor[5] falling on his knees, and they all with him, with watery cheeks commended them with most fervent prayers to the Lord. Then with mutual embraces and many tears they took their leave one of another; and it proved to be the last leave to many of them.

Then hoisting sail, with a prosperous wind they came in a short time to Southampton,[6] where they found the larger ship, which had come from London, lying ready with all the rest of their company. After a joyful welcome, and mutual congratulations, with other friendly entertainments, they began to talk about their

---

[3] Fourteen miles.

[4] **Delft-Haven** —A small port in the Netherlands, near Rotterdam.

[5] **Pastor.**—John Robinson.

[6] **Southampton** — *Where?*

business, and to dispatch it with the greatest speed, and also with their agents about the alteration of the conditions.[7]

Mr. Carver pleaded he was employed here at Southampton, and did not know what the other agent had done in London. Mr. Cushman answered that he had done nothing but what he was

A MODEL OF THE MAYFLOWER IN PILGRIM HALL, PLYMOUTH.

urged to do, partly on the ground of equity, but more especially by necessity, otherwise all had been dashed and many undone. And as to giving them notice at Leyden of this change, he could not omaccount of the shortness of the time, besides he knew it

---

[7] **Alteration of the conditions.** — The merchants at London who had agreed to assist the colonists with money wished the original conditions of the agreement at Leyden to be altered, and to this the agents consented.

would trouble and hinder the business which had already been too long delayed for the season of the year, which he feared they would find to their cost. But these things did not give any satisfaction at present.

Mr. Weston also came up from London to see them off and to have the conditions confirmed ; but they refused, and answered him that he knew right well that these were not according to the first agreement, neither could they yield to them without the consent of the rest that were left behind. Indeed, they had special instructions when they came away, from the chief of those who were left behind, not to do it. At this he was much offended, and told them they must expect to stand upon their own legs. So he returned in displeasure, and this was the first cause of discontent between them. And as they needed nearly one hundred pounds to clear things at their going away, he would not take order to disburse[8] a penny, but left them to shift for themselves as they were able. So they were forced to sell some of their provisions to stop this gap. They sold some three or four score firkins of butter, which commodity they could best spare, having provided too large a quantity.

All things being now ready, and every business dispatched, the company was called together. Then they distributed their company for either ship, as they considered best. They chose a governor and two or three assistants for each ship, to order the people by the way,[9] and to attend to the disposal of their provisions. This being done, they set sail about the 5th of August.

"The 'embarkation' took place at Delft-Haven. Delft-Haven is an unimportant seaport on the long line of the Dutch coast, yet it is worthy of remembrance, for it marks the march of man toward the future and toward freedom. On the morning of the 22d of July, of the year 1620, a few persons, on the quiet quay, knew that a small bark of sixty tons, called the Speedwell, was preparing for a voyage ; but whither and for what? She was no merchantman bound for gain, no privateer for plunder, no holiday sail for pleasure, no explorer for new continents."— *Motley.*

---

[8] **Disburse.**—*Meaning?*          [9] **By the way.**—On the passage.

## CHAPTER VIII.

### Their Departure from England and Voyage to America.

Being thus put to sea, they had not gone far before Mr. Reinolds, the master of the small ship,[1] complained that he found his ship so leaky that he did not dare go further out to sea until she was repaired. So Mr. Jones, the master of the larger ship, being consulted with, both resolved to put into Dartmouth and have her examined. Some leaks being found and mended, it was thought by the workmen and all that she was seaworthy and they might proceed without fear on their voyage. So with good hopes they put to sea again, imagining they could go comfortably on, and not expecting any more hindrances of this kind.

But it happened otherwise, for after they were gone to sea again about one hundred leagues from Land's End,[2] keeping together all the time, the master of the small ship complained that his ship was so leaky that he must bear up[3] or sink at sea, for they could scarcely free her with much pumping. So they consulted together again and resolved that both ships should back up again and put into Plymouth,[4] which accordingly was done. No special leak could be found, but it was judged to be the general weakness of the ship, and that she would not prove sufficient for the voyage. It was therefore decided to dismiss her and part of the company and proceed with the other ship. So after they took out such provisions as the other ship could well stow, and concluded what number and what persons to send back, they made another sad parting, one ship going back to London, and the other proceeding on her voyage.

---

[1] Speedwell.

[2] **Land's End.** — *Where?*

[3] **Bear up.** —To change the course of a ship when close-hauled, or sailing with a side wind, and make her run before the wind.

[4] **Plymouth, England.**

These troubles blown over, and now⁵ all being compact in one ship, they put to sea again with a prosperous wind, which lasted several days, and was some encouragement to them; yet according to the usual manner many were afflicted with seasickness. After they had enjoyed fair winds and weather for a season, they would often encounter cross winds, and meet with many fierce storms, with which the ship would be greatly shaken. This caused them some fear that the ship would not be able to perform the voyage. But upon consideration the master and others affirmed that they knew the ship was strong and firm under water.⁶ So they resolved to proceed. In some of these storms the winds were so fierce and the sea so high that they could not bear a knot⁷ of sail, but were forced to hull for days together. In one of them, as they lay in a fearful storm, a strong young man, coming upon one occasion above the gratings, was, by force of the waves, washed overboard. He kept hold of the topsail halyards,⁸ and was hauled up by the same rope to the edge of the water, and his life saved. In this voyage but one passenger died.

---

## CHAPTER IX.

### SEARCH FOR A LANDING.

But to omit other things that I may be brief, after long beating at sea they came to that land which is named Cape Cod,¹ which being reached and certainly known, they were not a little

---

⁵ **Now.**—Sept. 6.

⁶ **Under water.**—Below the water-line.

⁷ **Knot.**—A nautical mile. A term to indicate the progress of a vessel. The meaning here is, that the storms were so severe that the vessel could not carry any sail, but was driven before the wind, i.e., was forced to hull.

⁸ **Halyards.**—Ropes for hoisting and lowering the sails.

¹ **Cape Cod.**— *Where? Why so named?*

joyful.[2] After some deliberation among themselves and with
the master of the ship, they tacked about and resolved to steer
southward, the wind and weather being fair, to find some place
about Hudson River for their habitation. But after they had sailed
the course about half a day they fell among dangerous shoals and

roaring breakers, and were so far entangled therewith that they
thought themselves in great danger, and the wind dying away, they
decided to turn towards the Cape again. The next day they got
into the harbor, where they rode in safety. Being thus arrived
in a good harbor, and brought safely to land, they fell upon their
knees and blessed the God of heaven who had brought them over
the vast and furious ocean, and delivered them from all the perils

[2] The Mayflower dropped her anchor in the roadstead of what is now
Provincetown Harbor.

and miseries thereof, again to set their feet on the firm and stable earth, their proper element.

Having thus passed the vast ocean, and a sea of troubles before in their preparation,[3] they had now no friends to welcome them, nor inns to entertain or refresh their weather-beaten bodies, no houses or, much less, towns to repair to, to seek for succor.[4] It was winter, too, and they who know the winters of the country know them to be sharp and violent, subject to furious storms, dangerous for travel from place to place, much more for searching an unknown coast. Besides, what could they see but a hideous and desolate wilderness, full of wild beasts and wild men? If they looked behind them there was the mighty ocean which they had passed, and which was now a barrier and gulf to separate them from all the civilized world.

If it be said they had a ship to succor them, it is true; but what did they hear daily from the master and company?—that with their shallop[5] they should, with speed, seek out a place, at some neard istance, where they would be; for the season was such that he would not stir from thence till a safe harbor was discovered into which he might go without danger. Furthermore, the victuals were being consumed, but he must and would keep sufficient for themselves[6] and their return. What could now sustain them but the Spirit of God and His grace? May not the children of these fathers rightly say: "Our fathers were Englishmen who came over this great ocean, and were ready to perish in this wilderness; but they cried unto the Lord and He heard their voice, and looked on their adversity"?

---

[3] *To what is reference made?*

[4] The nearest English settlements were at Newfoundland and Virginia.

[5] **Shallop.**—A boat with sail, mast, and oars, but no deck. Some carried twenty or thirty men. (See illustration, p. 32.)

[6] **Themselves.**—The master and sailors.

## CHAPTER X.

### ARRIVAL AT CAPE COD.

HAVING arrived at Cape Cod on the 11th of November, necessity called them to seek a place for habitation. Whereupon a few of them volunteered to go by land and discover the nearest places. It was thought that there might be some danger in the attempt, yet seeing them resolute they were permitted to go, sixteen of them well armed, under the conduct of Captain Standish, having such instructions as were thought best. They set forth the 15th of November, and when they had marched about a mile by the seaside, they saw five or six persons with a dog coming towards them. These were savages ; but they fled into the woods, and the English followed them, partly to see if they could speak with them, and partly to discover if there might not be more of them lying in ambush. But the Indians, perceiving that they were followed, again forsook the woods, and ran away on the sands as hard as they could, so that our men could not come near them.

Afterwards the English directed their course towards the shore, for they knew it was a neck of land [1] they were to cross over, and so they at length got to the seaside, and marched to discover some river, and by the way found a pond of clear, fresh water, and shortly after a good quantity of clear ground where the Indians had formerly set corn,[2] and also found some of their graves. So the time assigned them having expired they returned to the ship, lest their friends should be concerned regarding their safety. They took with them part of the corn,

---

[1] Because of the explorations of Gosnold in 1602, and his maps.

[2] **Set corn.**—Planted fields of corn.

and buried up the rest. After this, the shallop being got ready, they set out again for the better discovery of the place.

The month of November having passed in these affairs, and much bad weather setting in, on the 6th of December they sent out their shallop again with ten of their principal men, and some seamen. After they were landed it grew late, and they made themselves a barricade with logs and boughs, as well as they could in the time, and sent out their sentinel and laid themselves to rest, in sight of the smoke of the fire that the savages made during the night. When morning was come they divided their company, some to coast along the shore in the boat, while the rest marched through the woods to see the land, and to find, if they could, any suitable place for a dwelling. So they ranged[3] up and down all day, but found no place that they liked.

When the sun set they hastened out of the woods to meet the shallop, which they signalled to come into a creek hard by. So they made a barricade, as they usually did every night, with logs, stalks, and thick pine-boughs, the height of a man, leaving it open to leeward, partly to shelter them from the cold and wind—making their fire in the middle and lying around it—and partly to defend themselves from the assaults of the savages, if they should surround them. Being very weary, they laid themselves down to rest. About midnight they heard a hideous cry, and their sentinel called "Arm, arm;" so they hurried themselves and shouldered their arms, and shot off a couple of muskets, and then the noise ceased. They concluded that it must be a pack of wolves, or other wild beasts; for one of the seamen told them he had often heard such noises in Newfoundland.

So they rested until about five o'clock in the morning. After prayer they prepared for breakfast, and it being the dawn of day it was thought best to commence carrying things down to the boat. Presently, all of a sudden, they heard a great and strange cry, which they knew to be the same voices heard in the night, though they varied their notes, and one of their com-

---

[3] **Ranged**.—*Meaning?*

pany being abroad came running in, and cried, "Men, Indians, Indians!" and at the same time arrows came flying among them. The cry of the Indians was dreadful, especially when

they saw our men running out of their rendezvous towards the shallop, to recover their arms. The Indians meanwhile were wheeling about on them. Not one of our men was either hit or hurt, although the arrows came close by them on every side, and some of their clothes, which hung up in the barricade, were shot through and through. Afterwards they gave God solemn thanks and praise for their deliverance, and gathered up a bundle of the arrows, and afterwards sent them to England by the master of the ship, and called that place "the first encounter."

From this place they departed, and coasted all along, but saw no place for a harbor. After some hours' sailing it began to snow and rain, and about the middle of the afternoon the wind increased and the sea became very rough. They broke their rudder, and it was as much as two men could do to steer with a couple of oars. But their pilot bade them be of good cheer, for he saw the harbor; but the storm increasing, and night coming on, they bore what sail they could to get in while they could see. But here they broke their mast in three pieces, and their sail fell overboard in a very heavy sea, so that they came near being cast away; yet they recovered themselves, and, having the tide with them, struck into the harbor.

Although it was very dark and rained hard, yet at last they got under the lee of a small island and remained there all night in safety. But they did not know this was an island[4] until morning. On Monday they sounded the harbor and found it fit for shipping; and marched into the land, and found many cornfields, and little running brooks. It was a place which they supposed to be fit for habitation; at least it was the best they could do, and the season and their present necessity made them glad to accept of it. So they returned to their ship again with this news to the people, which was a source of great comfort to them.

On the 15th of December they weighed anchor to go to the place they had discovered, and came within two leagues of it, but were compelled to bear up again; but the 16th day the wind became fair, and they arrived safely in this harbor.[5] Afterwards they took a better view of the place, and resolved where to pitch their dwelling, and on the 25th day began to erect their first house for common use, to receive them and their goods.

---

"December 11th, celebrated as the day of the landing of the Pilgrims at Plymouth. It corresponds to Dec. 21st, new style. By a singular error the 22d was supposed to be the true 'Forefathers' Day,' and for years has been duly observed as such."

---

[4] **Clark's Island.**—Named for the master's mate of the Mayflower, one of the exploring party. There is here a large boulder with the inscription, "On the Sabbath Day we rested."

[5] **Harbor.**—Plymouth.

## CHAPTER XI.

### The Remainder of the Year 1620.

I shall here turn back a little in my narrative and begin with a combination made before they came ashore, being the first foundation of their government in this place; occasioned partly by discontented and mutinous speeches that some of the strangers among them had let fall in the ship—that when they came ashore they would use their own liberty; for none had power to command them, the patent that they had being for Virginia, and not for New England, which belonged to another government, with which the Virginia company had nothing to do.

The form was as follows :

*In the name of God, Amen. We whose names are underwritten, the loyal subjects of our dread sovereign lord, King James, by the grace of God, of Great Britain, France, and Ireland, king, defender of the faith. etc., having undertaken, for the glory of God, and advancement of the Christian faith, and honor of our king and country, a voyage to plant the first colony in the northern part of Virginia, do by these presents solemnly and mutually, in the presence of God, and of one another, covenant and combine ourselves together into a civil body politic, for our better ordering and preservation and furtherance of the ends aforesaid ; and by virtue hereof, to enact, constitute, and frame such just and equal laws, ordinances, acts. constitutions and offices, from time to time, as shall be thought most meet and convenient for the general good of the Colony unto which we promise all due submission and obedience. In witness whereof we have hereunto subscribed our names at Cape Cod, November 11, in the year of the reign of our sovereign· lord, King James, of England, France, and Ireland the eighteenth, and of Scotland the fifty-fourth. An°: Dom. 1620.*

After this they chose, or rather confirmed, Mr. John Carver, a man godly and well approved amongst them, their Governor for that year. And after they had provided a place for their goods, or common store, which were long in unloading for want of boats, foulness of winter weather, and the sickness of many of them, and begun some small cottages for their habitations, as time would admit, they met and consulted about law and order, both for their civil and military government, as the necessity of their condition required.

That which was most sad and lamentable was, that in two or three months' time half of their company died, being infected with the scurvy and other diseases, which this long voyage and their lack of accommodations had brought upon them: so that two or three died in one day, and out of one hundred and odd persons hardly fifty remained. And of these during the time of greatest distress not more than six or seven were sound, who, to their commendation be it said, spared no pains either day or night, but with great labor and danger to their own health brought wood, made them fires, dressed them meat, made their beds, in a word did everything necessary for them; and all this was willingly and cheerfully done, without any grudging in the least, showing herein their true love unto their friends and brethren. A rare example, and one worthy to be remembered. Two of these seven were Mr. William Brewster, their reverend elder, and Myles Standish,[1] their captain and military commander, unto whom myself and many others were much beholden in our low and sick condition.

But I may not here pass by another remarkable passage not to be forgotten. The passengers were hurried ashore and made to drink water, that the seamen might have the more beer, and one[2] in his sickness desiring but a small can of beer, was answered

---

[1] Myles Standish was born in Lancashire, went over into the Low Countries when young, and was a soldier there, and there became acquainted with the church at Leyden. He was a man of small stature, but of unquestioned courage and resolution, and was for many years the captain of the colonists in all their warfare. He died in 1655.

[2] One.—Wm. Bradford.

that if he were their own father he should have none. Another lay scolding his wife, saying if it had not been for her he had never come on this unlucky voyage, and anon scolding his fellows, saying he had done this and that for some of them, he had spent so much, and so much, amongst them, and they were now weary of him, and did not help him in his need. Another agreed to give his companion all he had, if he died, to help him in his weakness; he went and got a little spice and made him a mess of meat once or twice, and because he did not die as soon as he expected, he went amongst his fellows, and swore the rogue would cheat him, and that he would see him choked before he prepared him any more meat; and yet the poor fellow died before morning.

All this time the Indians came skulking about them, and would sometimes show themselves afar off, but when any one attempted to approach them they would run away. Once they stole their tools where they had been at work and while they were gone to dinner. About the 16th of March a certain Indian came boldly among them and spoke to them in broken English which they could well understand but were astonished at. His name was Samoset; he told them also of another Indian whose name was Squanto, a native of this place, who had been in England [3] and could speak better English than himself. Being dismissed, after some time of entertainment and with gifts, he afterward came again, and five more with him, and they returned all the tools that had been stolen, and made way for the coming of their great Sachem, called Massasoit; who, about four or five days after, came with the chief of his friends and other attendants and with the aforesaid Squanto.

After friendly entertainment, and some gifts given him, they made a peace with Massasoit, which has [4] now continued for twenty-four years, in these terms:

---

[3] Squanto had been kidnapped by one Captain Hunt seven years before, and carried to England. He returned with an exploring party sent out by Sir Ferdinando Gorges.

[4] Bradford was writing this narrative in 1645.

1. That neither he nor any of his should injure or do hurt to any of their people.

2. That if any of his did any hurt to any of theirs, he should send the offender that they might punish him.

3. That if anything were taken away from any of theirs, he should cause it to be restored; and they should do the like to his.

4. If any did unjustly war against him, they would aid him; if any did war against them, he should aid them.

5. He should send to his neighboring confederates[5] to certify them of this, that they might not wrong them, but might be likewise comprised in the conditions of peace.

6. That when their men came to them, they should leave their bows and arrows behind them.

After these things he returned to his place called Sowams,[6] but Squanto continued with them. He directed them how to set their corn, where to take fish, and to procure other commodities, and was also their pilot to bring them to unknown places for their profit, and never left them until he died.

## CHAPTER XII.

### EVENTS OF 1621.

THEY now began to dispatch the ship which brought them over, and which lay[1] until about this time or the beginning of April. On the 14th of January the house which they had made for a general rendezvous by accident caught fire, and some were compelled to go aboard ship for shelter. Then sickness began to come amongst them, and the weather was so bad that they could not make any greater haste.

---

[5] **Confederates.**—Allies.
[6] **Sowams.**—Now the town of Warren, R. I.

[1] **Lay.**—Remained at anchor in the harbor.

In the month of April while they were busy about their seed, their Governor, Mr. John Carver, came out of the field very sick, it being a hot day; he complained greatly of his head, and lay down, and within a few hours became unconscious, so that he never spoke again, and died within a few days. Shortly after William Bradford was chosen Governor in his stead, and not being fully recovered from his illness, in which he had come near dying. Isaac Allerton was chosen to be an assistant to him. By renewed election every year, he continued several years in succession, which I here note once for all.

May 12th was the date of the first marriage[2] in the place, which, according to the laudable custom in the Low Countries in which they had lived, was considered best to be performed by the magistrate.

Having finished their business at home it was thought advisable to send some of their number to visit their new friend Massasoit, and to show him some gratitude in order to attach him to them. So on the 2d of July they sent Mr. Edward Winslow and Mr. Hopkins, with the aforesaid Squanto for their guide, to give him a suit of clothes, and a horseman's coat, with some other small things, which were kindly accepted; but they found but short commons,[3] and came home both weary and hungry. For the Indians used then to have nothing like so much corn as they have since the English have stocked them with their hoes, and seen to their industry in breaking up new grounds therewith.

They found Massasoit's place to be about forty miles distant, the soil good, and not many people, as there had been great mortality in these parts about three years before the arrival of the English, when thousands of them died—so many, in fact, that the living were not able to bury the dead, and their bones and

---

[2] **First marriage.**—Edward Winslow and Susannah White.

[3] **Short commons.**—A scanty supply of food. In the English universities the food provided for each student at breakfast is called his *Commons.* Hence food in general.

skulls were found in many places still lying above the ground. This party brought back word that a tribe of Indians called the Narragansetts lived on the other side of the great bay; that they were a strong people, many in number, living compact together, and had not been touched by this wasting plague.

Peace and acquaintance was pretty well established between the English and the natives about them; and another Indian called Hobomack came to live amongst them—a good strong man, and of importance for his valor and talents among the Indians,—who continued very faithful to the English until his death.

On the 18th of September they sent out their shallop to Massachusetts Bay with ten men, and Squanto for their guide and interpreter, to discover and view the bay, and trade with the natives; which they did, and found kind entertainment.

The people were much afraid of the Tarentins,[4] a people to the eastward, who used to come in harvest time and steal away their corn, and many times killed some of their number. They returned in safety and brought home a good quantity of beaver, and made a report of the place, wishing they had located there; but it seems that the Lord, who assigns to all men the bounds of their habitations, had appointed it for another use.

They now began to gather in the small harvest they had, and to fit up their houses and dwellings against the winter. They were well recovered in health and strength, and had all things in great plenty; for as some were employed in affairs abroad, others were engaged in fishing for cod, bass, and other fish, of which they caught a fair quantity, and of which each family had its share. All the summer there was no want. And now as winter approached, there began to come in store of fowl, with which this place did abound. Besides water-fowl, there was a great store of wild turkeys, of which they took many, and also stored a supply of venison. They also laid in a peck of meal a week to a person, or, now since harvest, Indian corn in the same proportion. This made many afterwards write their friends in England such glow-

---

[4] **Tarentins.**—Indians living beyond the Penobscot River.

ing accounts of the plenty they enjoyed; and they were not exaggerated, but true reports.

---

"The husbandry of the first summer had been prosperous on its small scale. The crop of peas failed, but the barley was 'indifferent good,' and there was 'a good increase of Indian corn.' Fish and game were abundant. By the autumn, seven substantial dwellings had been built. Health was restored. The Governor sent out a party to hunt, that so they might, after a special manner, rejoice together after they had gathered the fruit of their labors. This was the first celebration of the national festival of New England, the autumnal Thanksgiving."—*Palfrey.*

---

## CHAPTER XIII.

### THE ARRIVAL OF "THE FORTUNE" AND "THE CHARITY." TROUBLE WITH THE INDIANS.

### NOVEMBER, 1621.

ABOUT twelve months from the time of their own arrival, there came to them unexpectedly from England, in a small ship,[1] a party of thirty-five persons, among whom was Mr. Cushman. As these people came out as settlers in this plantation they were not a little rejoiced to find the colonists in such good condition, and their larders[2] abundantly supplied with provisions, for most of them were robust young men, and many of them wild enough to little consider whither they went or what they came for until they found themselves in the harbor of Cape Cod. When they were landed they had not so much as a biscuit among them, or any other food, neither had they any bedding, nor many clothes, only some sorry things[3] they had in their cabins—not even a pot or a pan in which to cook food. The plantation was glad of this

---

[1] **Small ship.**—The Fortune, of 55 tons.

[2] **Larders.**—*Meaning?*
[3] **Sorry things.**—*Meaning?*

addition of strength, but wished that many of them had been in better condition, and that all were better supplied with provisions; but that could not be helped.

By this ship Mr. Weston sent from England a long letter to Mr. Carver, the late Governor, now deceased, full of complaints and expostulations about former passages[4] at Southampton, and keeping the ship so long in the country, and returning her without lading. This ship, called the Fortune, was speedily dispatched, laden with good clapboard as full as she could stow, and two hogsheads of beaver and otter skins. The freight was estimated to be worth near five hundred pounds.[5] Mr. Cushman also returned with the ship, to make a personal report to the merchant adventurers.

After the departure of this ship, which did not remain over fourteen days, the Governor and his assistant having disposed of the new-comers as they best could, took an exact account of all their provisions, and proportioned the same to the number of persons, and found out that it would not hold out more than six months at half allowance, and hardly that. And they could not well give less this winter time till fish came in again. So they were presently put on half allowance, one as well as another, which began to be hard, but they bore it patiently.

Soon after this ship's departure the great people of the Narragansetts,[6] in a braving manner, sent a messenger unto them with a bundle of arrows tied with a great snake-skin, which their interpreters told them was a threat and a challenge.[7] Upon which the Governor with the advice of others sent them a round answer[8] that if they had rather have war than peace, they might begin when they pleased; they had done them no wrong, neither did

---

[4] **Passages.**—Transactions.

[5] **Five hundred pounds.** — *How many dollars?*

[6] The Narragansetts were a powerful and warlike tribe that inhabited nearly all the territory of what is now included in the State of Rhode Island. It is said that at one time they could muster above five thousand fighting men.

[7] **Threat and challenge.**—*Difference in meaning?*

[8] **Round answer.**—*Meaning?*

any fear them, nor should they find them unprovided: and by another messenger sent the snake-skin back with bullets in it; but they would not receive it, and so sent it back again.

This made them more careful to look out for themselves, so that they agreed to enclose their dwellings with a good strong pale,[9] and make flankers [10] in convenient places, with gates which they locked every night, and kept a watch.

Herewith I shall end this year. Only I shall remember one passage more, rather of mirth than of weight. On Christmas day the Governor called them all out to work, as was usual; but the most of this new company [11] excused themselves, and said it went against their consciences to work on that day. So he led away the rest and left them; but when they came home at noon from their work he found the new-comers in the streets at play, openly—some pitching the bar,[12] and some at stool-ball,[13] and similar sports. So he went to them and took away their implements, and told them that it was against his conscience that they should play and others work. If they made the keeping of it a matter of devotion, let them keep their houses; but there should be no gaming or reveling in the streets. Since which time nothing has been attempted in that way, at least openly.

Now [14] after a manner their provisions were wholly spent, and they looked hard for supply, but none came. But about the end of May they spied a boat at sea, which at first they thought was some Frenchman; but it proved to be a shallop which came from a ship which Mr. Weston and another had sent out fishing, at a place called Damarins Cove,[15] forty leagues to the eastward of

---

[9] **Pale** —Stakes for inclosing land.

[10] **Flankers.**—Forts.

[11] **New company.**—Those who came in the Fortune.

[12] **Pitching the bar** was a trial of strength and skill.

[13] **Stool-ball** was played by any number of persons. Each player had a stool which he set upon the ground, taking his place in front of it. The object was to throw the ball so as to hit the antagonist's stool, as in cricket, only the hands were used instead of bats.

[14] 1622.

[15] **Damarins Cove Islands.**—"West by north from Monhegan," off the coast of Maine.

them, where that year many more came fishing. This boat brought seven passengers and some letters, but no victuals or any hope of them. After this came another of his ships,[16] and brought letters dated April 10th.

All hopes in regard to Mr. Weston were laid in the dust, and all his promised help turned into empty advice, which they apprehended was neither lawful nor profitable for them to follow. And they were not only thus left destitute of help in their extreme want, having neither victuals nor anything else to trade with, but others were ready to glean what the country might have afforded for their relief.

During the summer they built a fort with good timber, both strong and comely, which was of good defense, made with a flat roof and battlements,[17] on which their ordnance[18] was mounted, and where they kept constant watch, especially in time of danger. It served them also for a meeting-house, and was fitted up for that purpose.

The welcome time of harvest now approached, but it did not amount to much in comparison with a full year's supply; partly because they were not well acquainted with the way of raising Indian corn, and because of their many other employments, but chiefly on account of their weakness.

It may be thought strange that these people should fall into these extremities in so short a time,[19] after being comfortably provided when the ship left them, and having the advantage of that portion of corn that was obtained by trade. It must needs be their great neglect, for they spent excessively whilst they had or could get it.

No supply was heard of, neither knew they when they might expect any. So they began to think how they might obtain a better crop than they had done, that they might not still languish in misery. And so they assigned to every family a tract of land according to the proportion of their number, only for

---

present use, and ranged [20] all boys and youth under some family. This had very good success, for it made all hands very industrious, and much more corn was planted than otherwise would have been by any means the Governor or any one else could use. Besides, it saved a great deal of trouble and gave far better satisfaction. The women now went willingly into the field to set corn, and took their little ones with them, a thing which they would formerly have declared themselves unable to do.

About the last of June a ship arrived [21] with Captain West, who had a commission to be Admiral of New England. He told the Governor that they spoke with a ship at sea, that was bound for this plantation with many passengers. About fourteen days after the ship referred to came in. It was called the Anne, and Mr. William Pierce was master of it. They brought about sixty persons to join the community, some of whom were very useful and became good members to the body, and some of them were the wives and children of those who were already here.

When these passengers saw their low and poor condition they were much daunted and dismayed, and according to their various dispositions were variously affected: some wished themselves in England again; others fell to weeping, fancying their own misery in what they now saw in others; others pitied the distress they saw their friends had long been in, and still were under: in a word, all were full of sadness.

By the time harvest was come, instead of famine, God gave them plenty, and the face of things was changed, to the rejoicing of the hearts of many. The effect of their careful planting was well seen; for all had very near enough to last the year, and some of the abler sort and more industrious had to spare, so that no general want or famine has been among them since.

"The situation of the colonists in the spring of 1623 was peculiarly distressing. The narrative of their sufferings is affecting and thrilling. By the time their corn was planted, their victuals were spent, and they knew

[20] **Ranged.** — *Meaning ?*  Compare with same word page 31, and note difference in meaning.          [21] The Plantation.

not at night where to have a bit in the morning; nor had they corn or bread for three or four months together. Elder Brewster lived upon shell-fish. Tradition affirms that at one time there was but a pint of corn left in the settlement, which being divided, gave to each person a proportion of five kernels. In allusion to this incident, at the bi-centennial celebration in 1820, when much of the fashion, wealth, and talent of Massachusetts had congregated at Plymouth, and orators had spoken and poets sung the praises of the Pilgrims; amidst the richest viands which had been pre-pared, *five kernels of parched corn* were placed beside each plate, a simple but interesting and affecting memorial of the distresses of those heroic and pious men who won this fair land of plenty and freedom and happiness, and yet at times were literally in want of a morsel of bread."—*Hist. of Mass.* (Barry).

---

## CHAPTER XIV.

### ARRIVAL OF "THE CHARITY."

### 1624.

THE time of the new election of their officers for the year having come, and the number of their people having increased, together with troubles, the Governor desired them to change the present incumbents,[1] and also to add more assistants to the Gover-nor, for the better carrying on of affairs. If it was any honor or benefit, it was fit that others should be made partakers of it; if it was a burden (as doubtless it was), it was but proper that others should bear it; and that was the end[2] of annual elections. The result was, that where there had been but one assistant, they now chose five, and afterwards increased them to seven.

Shortly after this Mr. Winslow came over, and brought a pretty good supply. The ship[3] came for fishing—a thing fatal to this plantation. He brought three heifers and a bull—the first begin-ning of any cattle in the land.

A letter from England shall better declare these things:

---

[1] Gov. Bradford was re-elected.    [3] The Charity.
[2] **End.**—Means *intention* in this place = " to that *end*."

Beloved Sir: We have now sent you, we hope, men and means for these things—fishing, salt-making,[4] and boat-making; if you can succeed in them your wants may be supplied. I pray you exert yourself to establish these kinds of business. Let the ship be fraught[5] as soon as you can, and sent to Bilbow.[6] This ship-carpenter is thought to be the fittest man for you in the land, and will no doubt do you much good. Let him have an absolute command over his servants. and such as you put to work with him. The salt-man is a skillful and industrious man: give him men who can quickly learn the mystery of it. The preacher we have sent is, we hope, an honest, plain man, though none of the most eminent and rare.

We have taken a patent[7] for Cape Ann. I am sorry there is no more discretion used by some in their letters hither. Some say you are starved in body and soul; others that the stories of the goodness of the country are gross and palpable[8] lies; that there is scarcely a fowl to be seen or a fish to be taken, and many like reports. I wish such discontented men were here again, for it is a misery when the whole state of the plantation is thus exposed to the passionate humors of some discontented men. And as for myself, I shall hinder in future some that would go.

I am sorry we have not sent you more things; but the truth is, we have been to such expense to victual the ship, provide salt and other fishing implements, that we could not provide other comfortable things, as butter and sugar. I hope the return of this ship and the James will put us in cash again. The Lord make you full of courage in this troublesome business, which now must be stuck unto, till God give us rest from our labors.

Farewell in all hearty affection,

Your assured friend,

Jan. 24, 1623. R. C.

---

[4] *How was the salt made?*

[5] **Fraught.**—*Meaning?*

[6] **Bilbow.**—Bilboa, a port in Spain.

[7] **Patent.**—An official document conferring special rights on a person or party.

[8] **Palpable.**—*Meaning?*

With regard to these objections, answers were then made unto them, and sent over at the return of this ship; which did so confound the objectors, that some confessed their fault, and others denied what they had said, and ate their words;[9] and some others have since come over again and here lived, to convince themselves sufficiently, both in their own and other men's judgment.

That they might increase their tillage to better advantage, they made suit[10] to the Governor to have some portion of land given them permanently, and not by yearly lot: for by that means that which the more industrious had brought into good culture (by much pains) one year, left it the next, and often another might enjoy it: so the cultivation of their lands was much slighted, and to less profit. Their request was granted. To every person was given only one acre of land, as near the town as might be, and they had no more until the seven years[11] had expired. The reason was, that they might be kept close together both for more safety and defense, and the better improvement of the general employments.

The ship which had brought this supply was speedily discharged, and with her master and company sent for fish to Cape Ann, of which place they had a patent.

## CHAPTER XV.

### LYFORD AND OLDHAM.

THE third important person which the letters before mention, was the preacher which they sent over, by name John Lyford, about whom and whose doings I must speak more fully, although I will abridge things as much as I can. When this man

[9] **Ate their words.**—*Meaning?*
[10] **Suit.**—Request.
[11] **The seven years.**—The time which they had agreed to hold all things in common.

first came ashore, he saluted them with more reverence and humility than is commonly seen, and indeed made them ashamed, he so bowed and cringed [1] unto them, and would have kissed their hands if they had allowed him: yea, he wept and shed many tears, blessing God that had brought him to see their faces; and admiring the things they had done in their wants, as if he had been made all of love, and the humblest person in the world.

After a short time he desired to become a member of the church here, and was accordingly received. He made a full confession of his faith, and blessed God for this opportunity of freedom and liberty to enjoy the ordinances of God in purity among his people, with many more such like expressions. I must here speak a word also of Mr. John Oldham, who was a copartner with him in his after courses. He had been a chief stickler [2] in the former faction, and an informer to those in England. He also desired that former things might be forgotten, and he be looked upon as one that desired to share with them in all things. Thereupon they showed all readiness to conduct themselves towards him in all friendliness, and called him to counsel with them in all important affairs, without any distrust.

Thus all things seemed to go on very comfortably and smoothly amongst them; but this did not last long.

When the ship was ready to go, it was observed that Lyford was long in writing, and sent many letters, and could not forbear from communicating to his intimates such things as made them laugh in their sleeves.[3] The Governor and some of his friends who knew how things stood in England, and what hurt these things might do, took a shallop and went out with the ship a league or two to sea, and called for all of Lyford's and Oldham's letters. Mr. William Pierce being master of the ship, and knowing well their evil dealing both in England and here, afforded

---

[1] **Cringed.**—*Meaning?*
[2] **Stickler.**—*Meaning?*
[3] **Laugh in their sleeves.**—To laugh privately or unperceived while pre- serving a grave or serious demeanor toward the person laughed at; originally by hiding the face in the wide sleeves of former times.

him all the assistance he could. He found about twenty of Lyford's letters, many of them long and full of slanders, and false accusations tending not only to their prejudice, but to the ruin and utter subversion [4] of the colonists. Most of the letters they let pass; of others they sent copies and kept the originals, lest he should deny them, and then they could produce his own hand against him.

The ship went out towards evening, and in the night the Governor returned. They were somewhat surprised at it, but after some weeks, when they heard nothing had been known, they thought the Governor had only gone to dispatch his own letters. The reason that the Governor and the rest concealed these matters the longer, was to let things ripen, that they might the better discover their intents and see who were their adherents.

As to Oldham, few of his letters were found, for he was so bad a scribe [5] that his writing was scarcely legible, yet he was as deep in the mischief as the other. Thinking that they were now strong enough, they began to pick quarrels with everybody. Oldham being called to watch according to order, [6] refused to come, fell out with the captain, called him a beggarly rascal, resisted him, and drew his knife at him; though the officer offered him no wrong, but with all fairness required him to do his duty.

To cut the matter short, it at length grew to this issue, that Lyford with his accomplices, without ever speaking one word to the Governor, church, or elder, withdrew themselves and set up a public meeting apart, on the Lord's Day; with sundry such insolent doings, too long here to relate, and began now publicly to act what they had long been plotting.

---

[4] **Subversion.**—*Meaning?*

[5] **Scribe.**—*Meaning?*

[6] **According to order.**—In his turn.

The colonists kept watch in regular order.

## CHAPTER XVI.

### Expulsion of Lyford and Oldham from the Colony.

It was now thought high time to prevent further mischief, and to call them to account; so the Governor called a court and summoned the whole company to appear. He then charged Lyford and Oldham with such things as they were guilty of. But they resolutely denied most things, and required proof.

Then Lyford's letters were produced and some of them read, at which he was struck mute. But Oldham began to rage furiously, because they had intercepted and opened his letters, and threatened them in very high language, and in a most audacious and mutinous manner stood up and called upon the people, saying, "My masters, where are your hearts? Now show your courage. You have often complained to me so and so: now is the time; if you will do anything, I will stand by you." He thought that every one that had soothed and flattered him, or otherwise in their discontent uttered anything unto him, would now side with him in open rebellion, but he was deceived, for not a man opened his mouth.

After their trial and conviction the court censured them to be expelled from the place; Oldham immediately, though his wife and family had liberty to stay all winter, or longer, till he could make provision to remove them comfortably. Lyford had liberty to stay six months. It was, indeed, with some eye to his release, if he carried himself well in the mean time, and his repentance proved sound. Lyford acknowledged his censure was far less than he deserved.

But what amazed all was, that after a month or two, notwithstanding all his former confessions, convictions, and public acknowledgments, both in the face of the church and whole company, with so many tears and sad censures of himself before God and men, he should commence to again justify what he had done. For secretly he wrote a second letter to the adventurers in England, in which he justified all his former writings.

In the spring of the year 1625, about the time of their election, Oldham came again amongst them; and though it was a part of his censure, for his former mutiny, not to return without leave, yet in his daring spirit he presumed to return without any leave at all, being prompted by the evil counsel of others. And not only so, but he suffered his unruly passion to run beyond the limits of all reason and modesty, insomuch that some strangers that came with him were ashamed of his outrage, and rebuked him; but all reproofs were but as oil to the fire, and made the flame of his anger greater. He called them all to naught,[1] in this his mad fury, and a hundred rebels and traitors, and I know not what. But in conclusion they committed him till he was tamer, and then appointed a guard of musketeers, which he was to pass through,[2] and every one was ordered to give him a thump with the butt-end of his musket. He was then conveyed to the water-side, where a boat was ready to carry him away.

I now come to Mr. Lyford. His time having expired, his censure was to take place. He was so far from answering their hopes by amendment in that time, that he had doubled his evil, as is before noted. The moderators with great gravity declared that the former matters gave them cause enough to refuse him, and to deal with him as they had done.

From hence Lyford went to Natasco,[3] in Massachusetts Bay, where Oldham also lived.

---

[1] **Called to naught.**—To be called of no account; to revile.

[2] Running the gauntlet.

[3] **Natasco.**—Nantasket, a peninsula near the entrance to Boston harbor.

## CHAPTER XVII.

### EVENTS OF 1626 AND '27. RETURN OF STANDISH. DISTRIBUTION OF LAND.

ABOUT the beginning of April, 1626, the colonists heard of Captain Standish's arrival,[1] and sent a boat to fetch him home and the things he had brought. He was welcome, but the news he brought was sad in many respects; not only in regard to former losses, which their friends had suffered, by which some were much disabled from giving any further help, and some dead of the plague, but also that Mr. Robinson, their pastor, was dead, which struck them with much sorrow and sadness. He further brought them word of the death of their old friend, Mr. Cushman.

At the usual season of the coming of ships, Mr. Allerton,[2] who had been sent to England the year previous, returned, and brought some useful goods with him, according to the order given him. For upon his commission he took up two hundred pounds, which he now got at thirty per cent. They got the goods safely home, which was of much comfort and content to the plantation.

The Governor and counsel had serious consideration about settling in reference to this new bargain, or purchase made, in respect to the distribution of things both for the present and

[1] Standish had been dispatched to England to learn what terms could be made with the adventurers toward closing their contract of service and partnership with the colonists.

[2] Allerton was sent to conclude the negotiations thus begun, and he succeeded. "For the sum of eighteen hundred pounds, payable in nine annual installments, the Adventurers were to release their contract. A partnership was now formed of all the men, under an agreement that the trade should be managed in the way of a joint-stock company."

future. So they called the company together, and conferred with them, and came to this conclusion, that the trade should be managed as before, to help to pay the debts. Therefore they resolved, for sundry reasons, to take in all amongst them that were either heads of families, or single young men of ability, and all such persons as were above named should be reputed and enrolled for purchasers; single free men to have a single share, and every father of a family to be allowed to purchase so many shares as he had persons in his family; that is to say, one for himself, and one for his wife, and one for every child that he had living with him. As for the servants, they were to have only what either their masters should give them out of theirs, or what their deservings should obtain from the company afterwards. Thus all were to be divided into single shares, and every one was to pay his part towards the purchase, according to his proportion, and all other debts which the profits of trade would not cover. This gave all good content. Then they agreed that every person or share should have twenty acres of land, besides the single acres they had already; and they appointed where to begin—first on one side of the town, and then on the other side in like manner, and so to divide it by lot.

There is one thing that occurred in the beginning of the winter before, which I have left for this place, that I may handle the whole matter together. There was a ship with many passengers in her and sundry goods bound for Virginia. They had lost themselves at sea, either by the incompetency of the master or his illness, for he was sick and lame of the scurvy, so that he could but lie in the cabin-door and give directions. They came near the shoals of Cape Cod, and about high-water touched upon a bar of sand that lies before it, and threw out an anchor. After the Governor was well informed by the messengers of their condition, he caused a boat to be got ready, and such things to be provided as they wrote for, and went himself also and carried some trading commodities. These persons remained at Plymouth until some time the next year before they could have passage to Virginia.

This year also they had letters and messengers from the Dutch plantation, sent to them from the Governor there, and written both in Dutch and French. The Dutch had traded in these southern parts some years before they came, but began no plantation here till four or five years after their coming.[4]

After this there were many passages between them both by letters and other intercourse, and they had some profitable commerce together for several years, till other occasions interrupted.

---

## CHAPTER XVIII.

KENNEBEC PATENT. INTERCOURSE WITH THE DUTCH. EXPULSION OF MORTON.

### 1628.

HAVING procured a patent for Kennebec, they now erected a house up in the river in the most convenient place[1] for trade, and furnished the same with commodities for that end, both winter and summer, not only with corn, but also with such other commodities as the fishermen had traded with them, as coats, shirts, rugs, blankets, biscuit, peas, and prunes; and what they could not have out of England, they bought of the fishing ships, and so carried on their business as well as they could.

This year the Dutch sent again unto them from their plantation both kind letters, and also diverse commodities, as sugar, linen cloth, Holland,[2] finer and coarser stuffs. But that which turned most to their profit in time was an entrance into the trade of wampum,[3] for they now bought about fifty pounds'

---

[3] The first permanent colonization of New Netherlands was in 1623.

[1] Where Augusta now stands.

[2] **Holland.** — A fine linen, first made in Holland.

[3] **Wampum** —Small beads made of different-colored shells, used by N. American Indians as money, and also wrought into belts as an ornament.

worth of it of them; and they told them how salable it was at their fort Orania,[4] and persuaded them they would find it so at Kennebec;·and so it came to pass in time, but it was two years before they could dispose of this small quantity, till the inland people knew of it; and afterwards they could scarce ever get enough for them, for many years together.

And strange it was to see the great alteration it made in a few years among the Indians themselves, for all the Indians of these parts, and of Massachusetts, had none or very little of it, but the sachems, and some special persons, who wore it for ornament. But after it grew thus to be a commodity in these parts, these Indians took to it also, and learned how to make it; for the Narragansetts gather the shells, of which they make it, from their shores. It has now continued as a commodity for the past twenty years, and may prove a drug in time. In the mean time it makes the Indians of these parts rich and powerful and also proud, and supplies them with pieces,[5] powder and shot, which no laws can restrain, and which, by reason of the baseness of sundry unworthy persons, both English, Dutch, and French, may turn to the ruin of many. Hitherto the Indians of these parts had no pieces, nor other arms except their bows and arrows; and for many years after they hardly dared to handle a gun, being very much afraid, and the very sight of one, though out of kilter,[6] was a terror to them.

And here I may take occasion to bewail the mischief that Morton[7] began in these parts, since base covetousness has now at length got the upper hand, and made this thing common : for, notwithstanding laws to the contrary, the Indians are fully supplied with both fowling-pieces, muskets, and pistols.

Some of the chief men of the straggling plantations, meeting

---

[4] Fort Orange, now Albany.

[5] **Pieces.**—Fire-arms.

[6] **Kilter.**—*Meaning ?*

[7] Morton was at Merry Mount, now Quincy, Mass., and he there was the leader of a company of riot-ous men, and, among other things, set up a May-pole, which the stern morality of the Puritans condemned, upon which occasion he broached a cask of wine, and held high revel and carousal.

together, agreed by mutual consent to solicit the Plymouth colonists, who were then stronger than them all, to join with them
to prevent the further growth of this mischief, and to suppress
Morton and his associates before they grew to greater strength.
So they first resolved to write to Morton, and in a friendly
and neighborly way admonish him, and sent a messenger with
their letters to bring his answer. But he was so high that he
scorned all advice, and asked who had to do with him?[8] He also
said that he had[9] and would trade pieces with the Indians, in spite
of all. They sent to him a second time, and bade him to recon-
sider. He answered in high[10] terms as before. Thereupon they
saw there was no way but to take him by force; and having
gone so far, it would make him far more haughty and insolent if
they should give up. So they mutually resolved to proceed, and
got the Governor of Plymouth to send Captain Standish and
some other aid with him to take Morton by force. They summoned him to yield, but he kept his house, and they could get
nothing but scoffs and scorn from him. But at length, fearing
they would do some violence to the house, he and some of his
crew came out. They brought Morton away to Plymouth,
where they kept him till a ship sailed from the Isle of Shoals[11]
for England.

This year Mr. Allerton brought over a young man for a
minister to the people here. His name was Mr. Rogers; but
they perceived, upon some trial, that he was crazed in his brain;
so they were obliged to be at the expense of sending him back
again the next year, and be at the loss of the money expended in
bringing him over.

Mr. Allerton in previous years had brought over some small
quantities of goods on his own risk, and sold them for his private
benefit, which was more than any man had yet attempted. But
because he had hitherto done them good service, and had sold

---

[8] **Who had to do with him?—**
"What business it was of theirs."

[9] **Had.—**Possessed.

[10] **High.—**Haughty.

[11] **Isle of Shoals.—***Where?*

his goods among the people of the plantation, whereby their wants were supplied, it [12] was passed over.

## CHAPTER XIX.

Mr. Allerton's Mistakes. Return of Morton, 1629–30.

### 1629.

That I may handle things together, I have put in this place the two companies that came from Leyden. Though they came at different times, yet they both came out of England this year. The former company, being thirty-five persons, were shipped in May, and arrived here about August. The latter were shipped in the beginning of March, and arrived here the latter end of May, 1630. The cost of bringing them over, as Mr. Allerton afterwards brought it in on account, came to above five hundred and fifty pounds, besides transporting from Salem [1] and the Bay, where they and their goods were landed. In addition to this expense, their friends and brethren here were to provide corn and provisions for them, till they could reap a crop, which was a long time away.

The Leyden people who thus came over, and sundry of the community, seeing and hearing how great the expense was likely to be, began to murmur at it, notwithstanding the burden lay on other men's shoulders.

Concerning Mr. Allerton's proceedings about the enlarging and confirming of their patent, both at home and at Kennebec, much time and money were spent, yet he left it unaccomplished this year, and came without it.

Mr. Allerton gave them great and just offense, in bringing over this year, for base gain, that unworthy man and instru-

---

[12] The expense of sending Rogers to England.

[1] **Salem.** — *Where?*

ment of mischief, Morton, who was sent home but the year before for his misdemeanors.   He not only brought him over, but to the town, and lodged him at his own house, where for a while he employed him as a scribe to do his business, till he was forced to send him away.   Morton went to his old nest, where it was not long before his misconduct gave them just cause to lay hands on him, and he was again sent prisoner by them to England, where he lay a good while in Exeter [2] jail.

I believe that private gain had somewhat to do in leading Mr. Allerton aside; yet I believe, and charity makes me hope, that, in the main, he intended to deal fairly with them.

Upon the consideration about the patent, it was concluded to send Mr. Allerton over this year, and this time with better success, for he obtained a grant under which the affairs of the colony were conducted for some years.

Mr. Allerton followed his affairs, and returned (1630) with his ship, the White Angel.   He was now no longer employed by the plantation; but his business was not ended until many years afterwards, nor well understood for a long time, to the great loss and vexation of the plantation, who in the end were, for peace' sake, forced to bear the unjust burden of the account, almost to their wrecking.

## CHAPTER XX.

### ROGER WILLIAMS.   SETTLEMENT ON THE CONNECTICUT RIVER.

### 1633.

THIS year Mr. Edward Winslow was chosen Governor.

Mr. Roger Williams,[1] a godly and zealous man, having many

---

[2] Exeter, England.

[1] "Roger Williams was a Welshman, educated at London and Cambridge, Eng.  He was the friend of Cromwell, Vane, and Milton.   It is to be noted in estimating Williams, that while detesting his opinions, men like Winthrop and Wins-

precious qualities, but very unsettled in judgment, came over
first to (Salem) Massachusetts, but upon some discontent left
the place and came hither, where he was entertained in a friendly
manner, according to our poor ability. He exercised his gifts
among them, and after some time was admitted a member of the
church. His teaching was well approved, and I am thankful to
him even for his sharpest admonitions and reproofs, so far as
they agreed with truth. He this year began to fall into some
strange opinions, and from opinion to practice, which caused
some controversy between the church and him, so that in the
end he became discontented, and left the church somewhat ab-
ruptly. Afterwards he sued for his dismissal to the church at
Salem, which was granted, with some caution. But he is to be
pitied and prayed for, and I desire the Lord to show him his
errors, and lead him back into the way of truth, and give him a
settled judgment and constancy, for I hope he belongs to the
Lord.

Having formerly had dealings with the Dutch, they were told
by them of a river, called by them the Fresh River, but now
known by the name of Connecticut, which they often commended
as a fine place both for habitation and trade, and wished them to
make use of it. But up to this time, being fully occupied
otherwise, they had let it pass. Afterwards there came a
company of banished Indians, who were driven from thence by
the power of the Pequods, who often solicited the English to go
thither, promising them much trade, especially if they would
keep a house there. And having now a good store of commodities, and needing to look out where they could better themselves,
they began to send that way to trade with the natives. They
found it to be a fine place, but had no great store of trade.
The Indians excused themselves on account of the season, and

low remained his friends. He was
generous when the several colonies
were in danger, and his exile was
remarkable for having proved the
salvation of the endangered plantations, for he alone was able to
control the intractable Narragansetts."—DRAKE.

the fear they were in because of their enemies.  They were the first English that both discovered that place[2] and built in the same, though they were little better than thrust out of it afterwards.

But the Dutch began now to repent, and hearing of the purpose and preparation of the English, endeavored to prevent them, by getting in a little before them, making a slight fort, and planting two pieces of ordnance, which threatened to stop their passage.  But they made a small frame of a house, and having a great new bark, they stowed their frame, and boards to cover and finish it, together with nails and all other provisions, in her hold.  When they came up the river, the Dutch demanded what they intended to do and whither they would go; they answered, up the river to trade.  So they passed along, and though the Dutch threatened them hard, they did not shoot them.  Coming to their place, the English built their house quickly, landed their provisions, left the companies appointed, and sent the bark home; they afterwards palisaded their house about, and fortified themselves better.  The Dutch sent home word of what was done; and in process of time they sent a band of about seventy men, in warlike manner, with colors displayed, to assault them; but seeing them strengthened, and that it would cost blood, they returned in peace.

This year many fell sick with an infectious fever, and upwards of twenty persons died, men and women, besides children.  This disease also swept away many of the Indians from all the adjoining places.

---

[2] What is now the town of Windsor, on the Connecticut.

## CHAPTER XXI.

### Scourge of Small-pox among the Indians.

### 1634.

I AM now to relate some strange and remarkable passages. There was a company of people lived in the country, up above on the Connecticut River, a great way from their trading-house, who were enemies to those Indians who lived about them, and of whom they stood in some fear. Three or four Dutchmen went up in the beginning of winter to live with them, to get their trade, and prevent them from bringing it to the English. But their enterprise failed; for the Indians were visited with a great sickness, and such mortality, that out of a thousand above nine hundred and a half of them died, and the Dutchmen almost starved before they could get away, being detained by ice and snow. But about February they, with much difficulty, reached their trading-house, being almost dead with hunger and cold.

Those Indians who lived about the trading-house also fell sick of the small-pox, and died most miserably. The condition of these people was so lamentable, and they fell down so generally with this disease, that they were in the end not able to help one another to make a fire, to fetch a little water to drink, nor any to bury the dead; but would strive as long as they could, and when they could procure no other means to make fire, they would burn the wooden dishes and trays they ate their meat in, and their very bows and arrows. Some would crawl out on all-fours to get a drink of water, and die by the way.

But those of the English house, though at first they were afraid of the infection, yet seeing their woful and sad condition, and hearing their pitiful cries and lamentations, had compassion on them, and daily fetched them wood and water, and made them fires, got them victuals whilst they lived and buried them when they died. Few of them escaped, notwithstanding they did what they could for them, to their own hazard. The chief sachem himself died, and almost all his friends and kindred. But not one of the English was so much as sick, or in the least measure tainted with the disease. And this mercy which they showed them was kindly taken, and thankfully acknowledged by all the Indians that knew or heard of it, and the people here much commended and rewarded them for it.

## CHAPTER XXII.

### EVENTS FROM 1635-1645.

MR. WINSLOW [1] was very welcome to them in England, and the more in regard of the large return he brought with him, which came all safe to their hands, and was well sold.

Mr. Edward Winslow was chosen Governor this year, 1636.

This year two shallops going from Massachusetts colony to Connecticut with the goods of such as removed thither were cast away in an easterly storm while coming into this harbor by night. The boatmen were lost, and the goods were driven all along the shore, and strewed up and down at high-water mark. But the Governor caused them to be gathered up and drawn together, by which means most of the goods were saved, and restored to the owners.

In the spring of 1637 the Pequods fell openly upon the English at Connecticut, and killed several of them as they were at work in the fields, both men and women, and went away in great pride and triumph, with many high threats. They also assaulted a strong and well-defended fort at the river's mouth;

---

[1] Mr. Bradford omits to record his own elections. He was chosen Governor this year, 1635.

and though they did not succeed, yet it alarmed and astonished the colonists.

This year, 1638, Mr. Thomas Prince[2] was chosen Governor.

It pleased God in these times so to bless the country with such emigration of people into it, that it was much enriched, and cattle of all kinds stood at a high price for several years together.

I am to begin this year, 1643, with what was a matter of great sadness and mourning unto all. About the 18th of April their reverend elder, and my dear and loving friend, Mr. William Brewster, died. He was nearly, if not quite, fourscore years of age when he died. He had this blessing added by the Lord to all the rest, to die in his bed, in peace, in the midst of his friends, who mourned and wept over him, and ministered what help and comfort they could unto him, and he in turn comforted them whilst he could. His sickness was not long, and until the last day thereof he did not wholly keep his bed.

By reason of the plottings of the Narragansetts, ever since the Pequod war, the Indians were drawn into a general conspiracy against the English in all parts, as was partly discovered the year before, and now made more plain and evident by the free confessions of sundry Indians upon several occasions, which gave opportunity to understand the truth thereof and to think of means to prevent their conspiracy. This made them enter into nearer union and confederation.

Mr. Edward Winslow was chosen Governor for 1644. Many having left this place by reason of their finding better accommodations elsewhere, the church began to consider whether it were not better jointly to remove to some other place than to be thus weakened. Many meetings and much consultation were held hereabout, and different opinions were expressed. Some were for

[2] Thomas Prince came to the colony in 1621, in the ship Fortune. He was one of the first settlers at Eastham, 1644, and afterward returned to Plymouth. He was chosen Governor in 1634, 1638, and not again until 1657, and continued in that office by renewed elections sixteen consecutive years, till his death in 1673.

staying together in this place, alleging that men might live here if they would be content with their condition; and it was not so much for want or necessity that they removed, as for the enriching of themselves. Others were resolute upon removal. The greater part consented to a removal to a place called Nawsett,[3] which had been superficially viewed, and the good-will of the purchasers, to whom it belonged, obtained. And thus was this poor church left, like an aged mother, grown old and forsaken of her children.

In 1645 the commissioners were called to meet together at Boston, before their ordinary time—partly in regard to some differences between the French[4] and the Government of Massachusetts, and partly about the Indians, who had broken the former agreements about the peace concluded the last year.

A treaty and agreement betwixt the commissioners[5] of the United Colonies and the sagamores[6] and deputy of Narragansetts and Niantic Indians was made and concluded. Two Indians acquainted with the English language assisted therein; they opened and cleared the whole treaty, and every article, to the sagamores and deputy there present.

And the war at this time was stayed and prevented.

---

[3] Eastham.

[4] **French.**—In Acadia.

[5] The commissioners of the United Colonies came from Connecticut, Plymouth, and New Haven to Boston, and a New England Confederation was formed. Thus the first attempt was made at the Federal system, which more than a century later became the central principle in the formation of the United States.

[6] Chiefs.

www.ingramcontent.com/pod-product-compliance
Lightning Source LLC
Chambersburg PA
CBHW021523090426
42739CB00007B/746